We live in a world filled with many different countries and diverse cultural, religious and ethnic groups. As we grow up, we learn how it feels to be accepted, or "fit" in a group. But we must also learn what to do if in certain situations we do not fit in. Our family hopes that our stories help you to learn how you can decide when it's best for you to fit in and when it can be better "not to fit in"

Hi, my name is Ronald.
When I started 2nd grade,
I made two friends and I fit in!

By 5th Grade my friends and I had formed our own group.
It was fun for us but not for the kids who didn't fit in...

In 8th grade, some kids fit in, but I didn't.
That felt sad, but I it gave me time to focus on the things that were important to me
like music, sports and school.

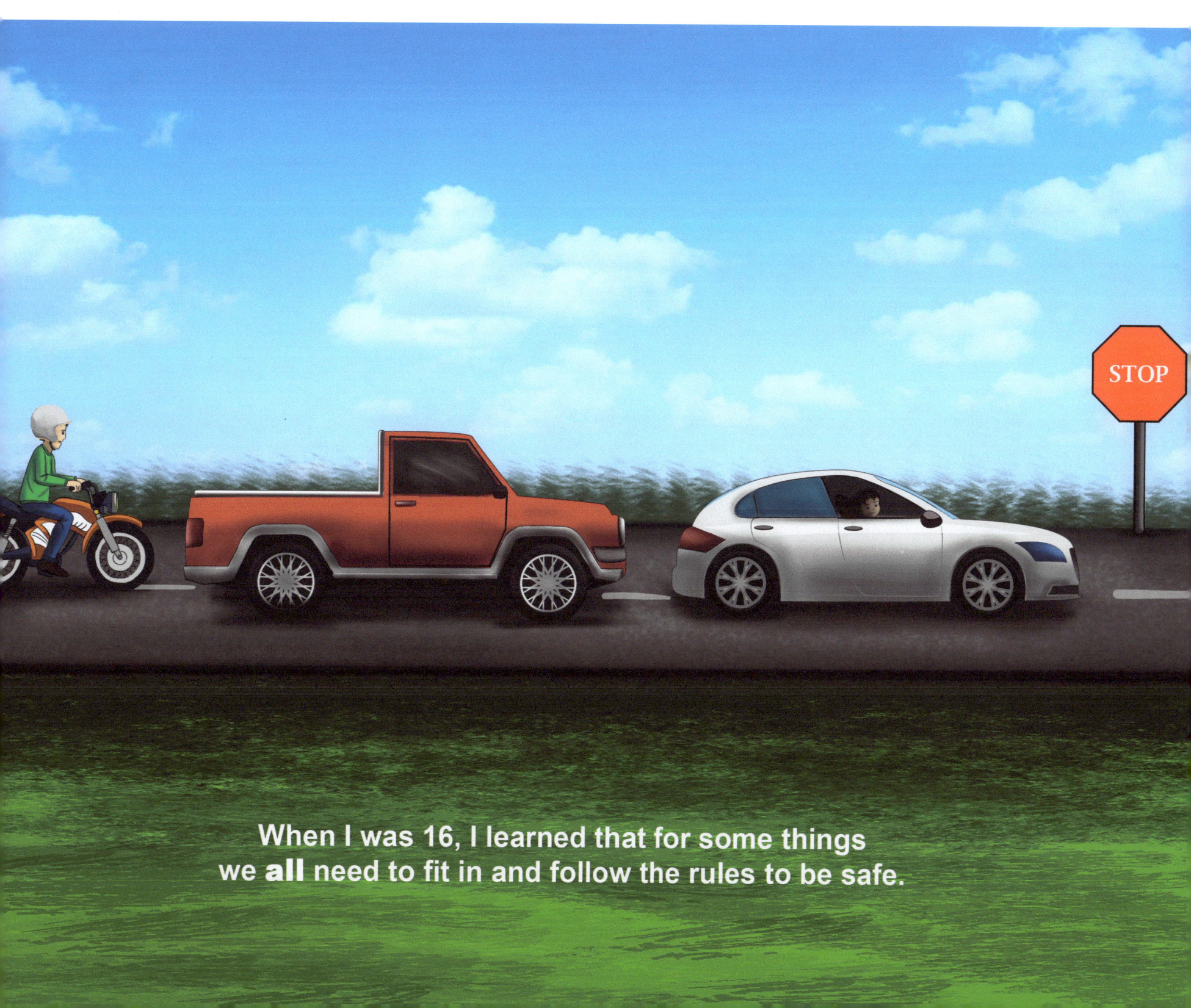

When I was 16, I learned that for some things
we **all** need to fit in and follow the rules to be safe.

When I was 17, I worked at a factory after school and learned that sometimes it can be good NOT to fit in....

In college, I met other kids who didn't fit in.
We made our own group where anyone
could fit in!

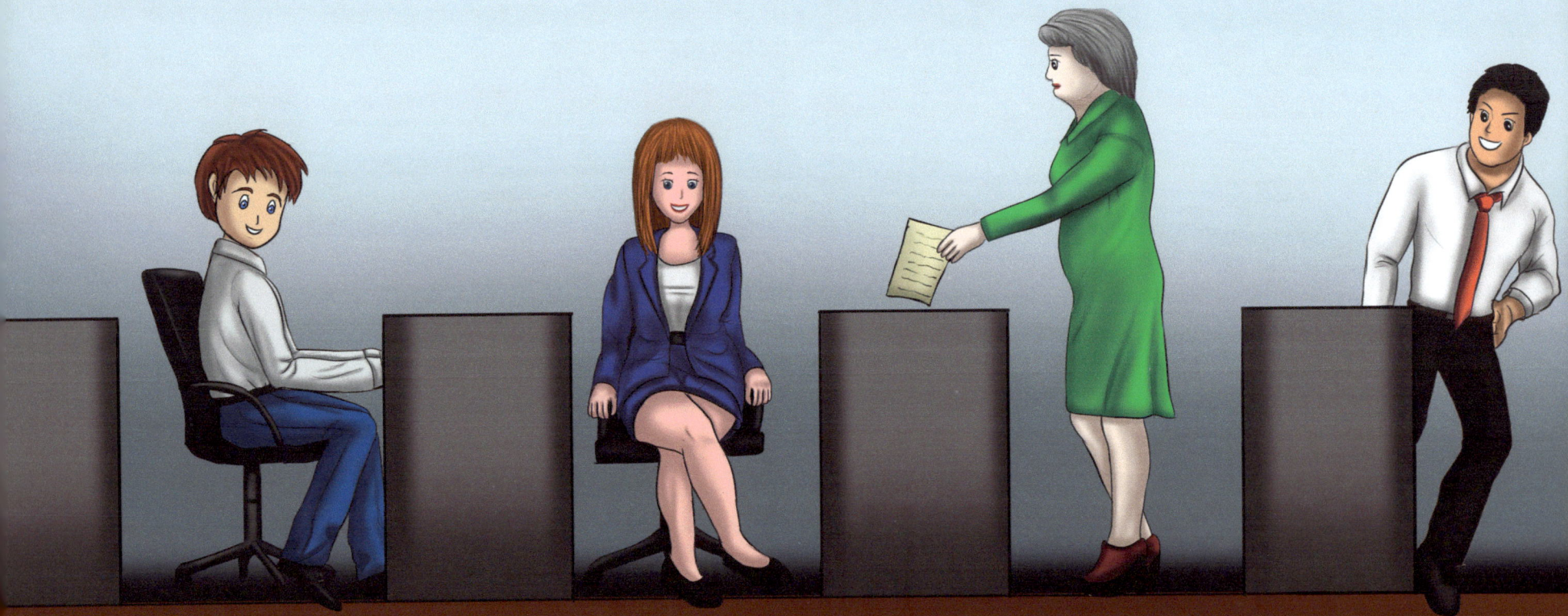

When I started work at a company, I
needed to learn so I knew I had to fit in.

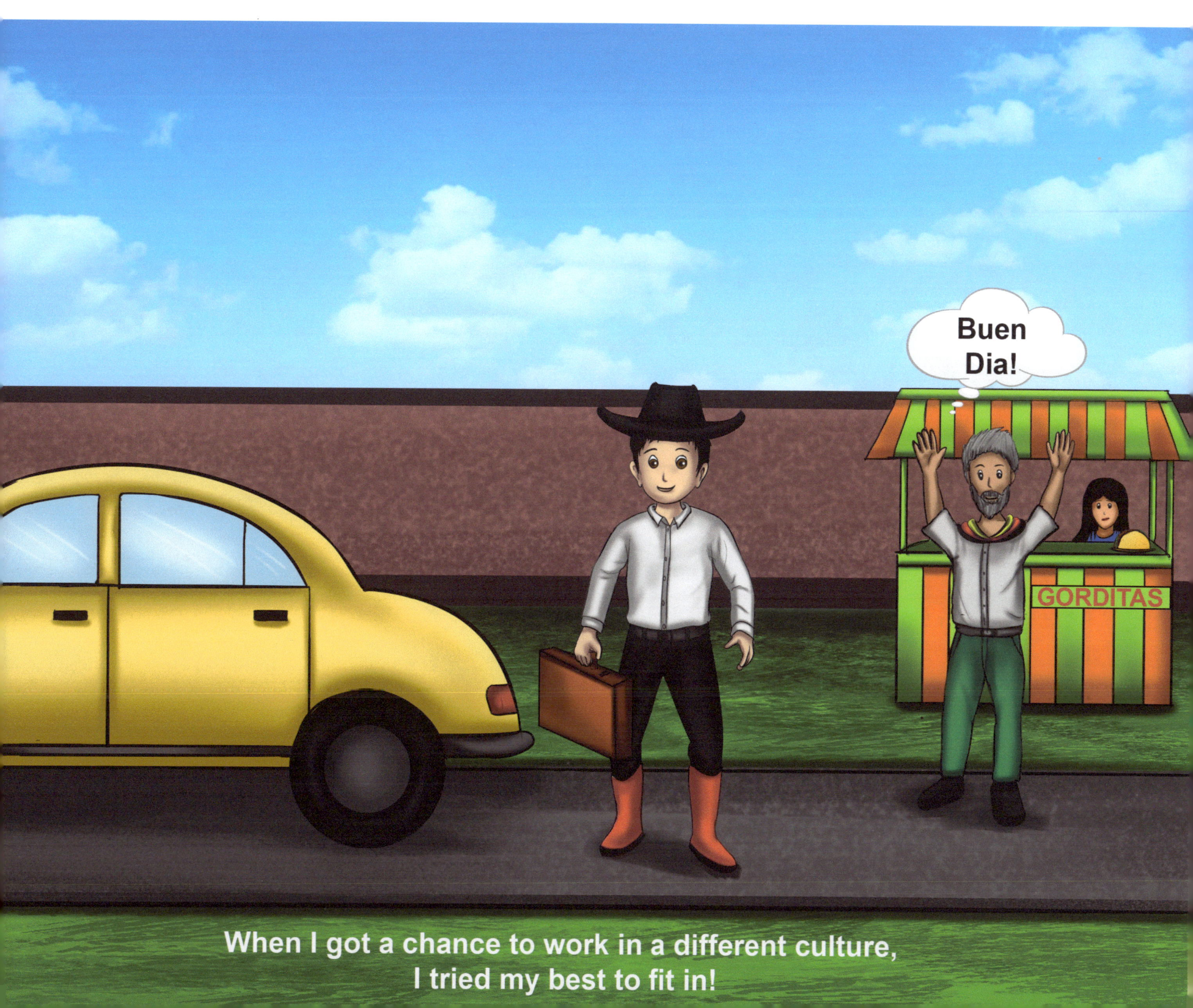

When I got a chance to work in a different culture,
I tried my best to fit in!

One day Ronald met Laura, They fit together and fell in love. They knew that they both had found their match and decided to get married !

We now have three boys and we teach them everything that we can!

We teach them to accept everyone and to make each person feel like they fit in. We all know how it feels not to fit in...we teach them empathy.

O's

We teach them that they won't always fit in. Sometimes that can feel sad and other times it can feel good, but they can decide when fitting in is right for them!

THE END